MUD TURTLE PET OWNER'S MANUAL

A complete guide to mud turtles, habitats, breeding, care, management and more included

By

Dr James L. King

Table of Contents

Introduction

Chapter 1
Mud turtle species

Mud turtles, often called African mud turtles or East African box turtles, are a fascinating group of reptiles known for their unique behavior and habitat preferences. This article aims to explore various species of mud turtles, their natural habitats, and which ones are suitable as pets.

1. Introduction to mud turtles

Mud turtles are small to medium-sized turtles belonging to the genus Pelusios, which is part of the family Pelomedusidae. These turtles are found primarily in sub-Saharan Africa and are known for their distinctive appearance, with a domed shell, webbed feet, and a preference for aquatic environments.

2. Common Mud Turtle Species

There are several species of mud turtles, each with their own characteristics and range. Some of the most commonly encountered species include:

A. Pelusios castaneus (African helmeted turtle)

- TThis is one of the most common mud turtle species and is known for its striking red or brown shells.
- They are often found in a wide range of habitats, from rivers and ponds to marshes and estuaries.
- African helmeted tortoises are not suitable as pets due to their size andspecific housing requirements.

B. Pelusios sinuatus (East African serrated mud turtle)

- These turtles have a serrated shell and are found in a variety of aquatic habitats.
- They are known for their distinctive saw-like edges on their carapace.
- Although they are interesting to watch, they are not generally kept as pets.

C. Pelusios subniger (African black mud turtle)

- They are smaller mud turtles with a dark colored shell.
- They are often found in muddy, slow-flowing rivers and wetlands.
- African black mud turtles are sometimes kept as pets, but they require specific care.

D. Pelusios adansonii (African softshell turtle)

- This species has a flattened soft shell appearance and a more aquatic lifestyle.
- They are often found in rivers, lakes and other bodies of fresh water.
- African softshell turtles are not generally kept as pets due to their special needs.

3. Housing preferences

Mud turtles are semi-aquatic creatures, meaning they spend a significant portion of their lives in or near water. Their habitat preferences vary by species, but generally include:

- Slow-flowing rivers
- Lakes and ponds
- Marshes and swamps
- Estuaries and coastal areas
- Muddy or sandy substrates for burrowing

4. Suitable Mud Turtle Species as Pets

Although mud turtles can be intriguing, not all species are suitable for captivity. It is crucial to consider the following factors when determining which species may be suitable as pets:

A. Size:
Some species of mud turtles can grow quite large, which can be a challenge for many keepers. Smaller species are more manageable for home enclosures.

B. Availability: Availability of specific species may vary by region. Some may be difficult to find from reputable sources.

C. Legal considerations: Make sure you are not violating any local, state or national laws by keeping a particular species as a pet.
d. Care Requirements:

Different species have different care needs. Research the specific requirements of the species you are interested in.

E. Conservation state:
Consider the conservation status of the species. Captive breeding and responsible ownership can contribute to the conservation of certain species.

5. Species adapted to captivity
One species of mud turtle often considered suitable for captivity is the African black mud turtle

(Pelusios subniger). They are smaller, making them more manageable for home enclosures. Here are some key characteristics and care guidelines for this species:

Appearance:
- African black mud turtles have a carapace length of 5 to 6 inches on average.
- They have a dark blackish-brown shell with subtle markings.

Habitat and environment:
- These turtles thrive in freshwater habitats, such as slow-moving rivers and ponds.
- A suitable enclosure should include both a basking area and a swimming area.

Diet:
- Their diet consists mainly of aquatic plants, insects and small aquatic invertebrates.
- A varied diet is essential to their well-being.

Temperature and lighting:

- Maintain an appropriate temperature in the basking area, usually around 85 to 90°F (29 to 32°C).
- Provide access to UVB lighting to support their calcium metabolism.

Compatibility

- African black mud turtles can be kept together, but watch for aggressive behavior.
- Avoid keeping them with other turtle species as they may not tolerate competition for resources.

Legal considerations

Always check local and state regulations to ensure you can legally keep African black mud turtles as pets.

In conclusion, mud turtles are a diverse group of reptiles, each with unique characteristics and habitat preferences. When considering them as pets, it is essential to research the specific species you are interested in and ensure their care requirements match your capabilities and local regulations. The African black mud turtle is one of the species adapted to captivity, but responsible ownership and dedication to meeting its needs is paramount to the well-being of these fascinating creatures. Always prioritize the welfare of these animals and consider the conservation implications of your decision to keep them as pets.

Chapter 2
Habitat configuration

Creating suitable habitat for mud turtles is essential for their health and well-being. In this detailed guide, we will explore the different aspects of designing an ideal enclosure for these unique reptiles. A well-constructed habitat will provide the right substrate, maintain appropriate temperature and humidity levels, and provide an environment that mimics their natural habitat. This guide will cover these items in depth to help ensure your mud turtle thrives in captivity.

Section 1: Substrate Selection

Substrate, or the material that covers the floor of the enclosure, plays a crucial role in replicating a natural environment for mud turtles. Here are some factors to consider when choosing substrate:

1.1 Types of substrates

Mud turtles are semi-aquatic reptiles, so the substrate should be a combination of terrestrial and aquatic areas. Common substrate types include:

A. Aquatic plants and gravel

In the water area of the enclosure, use aquatic plants and gravel to imitate a pond or riverbed.

The water part should be shallow, allowing the turtle to enter and exit easily.

B. Mixture of earth and sand

Create a terrain with a mixture of dirt and sand. This replicates the muddy banks and shorelines that mud turtles naturally inhabit.

Make sure the substrate is deep enough for burrowing behavior.

C. Flat rocks and hiding places

Provide flat rocks for basking and hiding places for added safety. Mud turtles like a mix of exposed and sheltered areas.

1.2 Substrate depth

The depth of the substrate is crucial. Mud turtles are known for their burrowing and digging behavior, so make sure the land area has sufficient depth to allow them to dig comfortably. A depth of at least 6 to 8 inches (15 to 20 cm) is recommended to allow for burial.

1.3 Substrate maintenance

Maintain and clean the support regularly. Remove trash, uneaten food, and debris from the enclosure to keep it hygienic.

Section 2: Temperature Regulation

Mud turtles are ectothermic, meaning they rely on external sources to regulate their body temperature. Maintaining a good temperature is vital for their health.

2.1 Rest area

Create a designated resting area within the enclosure. This area should receive direct sunlight or be equipped with appropriate heating and lighting elements.

2.2 Temperature gradient

Allow for a temperature gradient inside the enclosure. This means that one side of the habitat should be warmer (the basking area) while the other side remains cooler. The temperature gradient allows the turtle to move to the area that suits its needs at any time.

2.3 Recommended temperatures

Recommended temperature ranges for mud turtles are:

1. Basking zone: 85-90°F (29-32°C)
2. Coldest side: 70-80°F (21-27°C)

2.4 Heating and lighting

To maintain these temperatures, consider the following:

A. Heat lamps: Use heat lamps or ceramic heat emitters to provide heat to the basking area.
Make sure the heat source is securely mounted to avoid accidental contact with the turtle.

b. UVB lighting: Provide UVB lighting in the enclosure to support calcium metabolism and overall health of the turtle. Position the UVB lamp according to the manufacturer's recommendations.

2.5 Temperature monitoring

Use thermometers to monitor temperatures in different areas of the enclosure. This ensures that basking areas and cooler areas are within recommended ranges.

Section 3: Humidity Control

Mud turtles come from very humid environments and it is essential to replicate these conditions in captivity.

3.1 Housing humidity

Maintain an appropriate humidity level in the enclosure, particularly at ground level. Consider the following:

A. Soil moisture:

1. Keep the soil of the terrestrial area moderately moist, similar to the muddy banks of their natural habitat.
2. Mist the soil regularly to maintain humidity.

B. Water area:

1. The water area should also contribute to the overall humidity of the enclosure.
2. Make sure the water is clean and refreshed regularly.

3.2 Hydration

Mud turtles absorb water through their skin and cloaca, so access to clean water is essential. The aquatic space must allow the turtle to completely immerse itself in order to hydrate and soak up water according to its needs.

Section 4: Water Characteristics

As semi-aquatic reptiles, mud turtles need aquatic space in their enclosure. Creating a suitable water feature is essential.

4.1 Size of the body of water

The size of the water area should be large enough to allow the turtle to swim, soak and regulate its body temperature. The depth of the water area can vary, but it should be shallow enough that the turtle can touch the bottom and climb out comfortably.

4.2 Filtration and cleanliness of water

Make sure the water remains clean and free of contaminants. Use a filtration system to maintain water quality and change some of the water regularly.

4.3 Water temperature

The water temperature should be close to the ambient temperature of the enclosure. Mud turtles need access to water that is neither too cold nor too hot.

Section 5: Shelter and Hiding Places

Mud turtles like sheltered places where they can feel safe. Create hiding places within the enclosure to meet this need.

5.1 Natural hiding places

Use flat rocks, logs or plants to create natural hiding places. These areas allow the turtle to retreat and feel safe.

5.2 Sheltered from the elements

Provide shelter from extreme weather conditions if the enclosure is outdoors. Mud turtles are sensitive to sunlight and cold temperatures.

Section 6: Diet and Feeding Areas

An essential aspect of habitat layout is providing suitable foraging areas and a balanced diet.

6.1 Feeding areas

Designate specific areas for feeding to prevent food from contaminating the substrate. Use shallow dishes or platforms to place their food.

6.2 Diet

Mud turtles are herbivores and mainly consume aquatic plants, vegetables and some fruits. A balanced diet is essential to their health.

6.3 Feeding schedule

Offer food regularly, but avoid overfeeding. Provide a variety of leafy greens and vegetables to ensure a balanced diet.

Section 7: Environmental Enrichment

Mud turtles benefit from environmental enrichment to prevent boredom and encourage natural behaviors. Consider the following:

7.1 Decor and plant life

Add live or artificial plants to the enclosure to create a more natural environment. These also provide hiding places and contribute to humidity.

7.2 New objects

Occasionally introduce new items or items for the turtle to explore. This may include rearranging the decor or adding safe, non-toxic items.

Section 8: Social and Compatibility

Mud turtles can be raised alone or in groups, depending on the space available and the temperament of the individuals.

8.1 Solitary or group accommodation

Some mud turtles tolerate the presence of others, while others prefer solitude. Observe their behavior and interactions to determine the best arrangement.

8.2 Compatibility

If you keep several turtles, make sure they are similar in size and that there are no aggressive individuals in the group. Allow enough space to avoid territorial conflicts.

Section 9: Enclosure Maintenance

Proper habitat maintenance is crucial to the well-being of mud turtles.

9.1 Cleaning

Clean and disinfect the enclosure regularly. Remove trash, uneaten food and any contaminated substrate.

9.2 Water quality

Make sure the water in the aquatic area is clean and well filtered. Change some of the water regularly to maintain water quality.

Section 10: Legal Considerations

Before setting up an enclosure for mud turtles, be aware of any legal regulations or restrictions regarding keeping them as pets in your area. Be sure to follow all local, state and national laws.

In conclusion, creating a suitable habitat for mud turtles is crucial to their health and happiness in captivity. It is essential to replicate their natural environment with suitable substrate, temperature and humidity levels, as well as providing them with access to water, hiding places and a balanced diet. Regular maintenance and environmental enrichment are essential to keeping these unique reptiles healthy and content in their enclosure. Always prioritize the welfare of your mud turtle and ensure your facility meets legal requirements to provide them with the best possible care.

chapter 3
Diet and nutrition

Creating a well-balanced diet for mud turtles is essential for their overall health and longevity in captivity. Mud turtles are herbivorous reptiles and feed primarily on a variety of plants and vegetables. In this comprehensive guide, we'll explore the dietary needs of mud turtles, including their preferences, nutritional needs, and dietary guidelines. Understanding their dietary needs is essential to providing the best care for these unique reptiles.

Section 1: Mud Turtle Diet Overview

Mud turtles, belonging to the genus Pelusios, are primarily herbivorous in nature. Their diet consists primarily of plant matter, such as aquatic plants, leafy greens, and some vegetables. Good nutrition is essential to their well-being and it is important to imitate their natural diet as closely as possible.

Section 2: Natural Food in the Wild

Understanding what mud turtles eat in the wild is a fundamental step in replicating their diet in captivity. In their natural habitat, mud turtles consume:

2.1. Aquatic plants : Mud turtles feed on a variety of aquatic plants found in their habitat, such as water lilies, water hyacinths, and various submerged aquatic vegetation.

2.2. Leafy greens: They also graze on terrestrial vegetation near water sources, including grasses, clover, and other leafy greens.

2.3. Fruits and vegetables: Although most of their diet is plant-based, mud turtles may occasionally eat fruits and vegetables, such as berries and leafy greens.

Section 3: Nutritional Needs

To maintain the health of mud turtles in captivity, it is important to understand their nutritional needs.

Here are some key nutrients and components of their diet:

3.1. Fibre:A diet rich in fiber is essential for good digestion. Mud turtles need fiber to help them process the plant matter they consume.

3.2. Calcium: Calcium is crucial for shell health. Insufficient calcium intake can lead to shell deformations.

3.3. Phosphorus: While mud turtles require phosphorus for growth, an excessive phosphorus-to-calcium ratio can negatively affect calcium absorption.

3.4. Vitamins: Get a variety of vitamins through a diverse diet, including vitamin A, which is important for eye health.

3.5. Protein: Although mud turtles are herbivores, they still need protein. Most of their protein comes from plants.

3.6. Hydration: Mud turtles absorb water through their skin, so access to clean water is vital.

Section 4: Appropriate Foods

Selection of appropriate foods is crucial to meeting the nutritional needs of mud turtles. Here are some recommended foods:

4.1. Aquatic plants :
- Water lettuce
- Water hyacinth
- duckweed
- Anacharis

4.2. Leafy greens:
- Green cabbage
- Mustard greens
- Dandelion leaves
- Other
- Romaine lettuce (in moderation)

4.3. Vegetables:
- Squash
- Courgettes
- Carrots (in moderation)
- peppers
- Cucumber

4.4. Fruits (occasionally):

- Berries (e.g. strawberries, blueberries)
- Apple (in moderation)
- Banana (in moderation)

Section 5: Feeding Guidelines

Providing an appropriate diet is not limited to offering the right foods. Here are some feeding guidelines to follow:

5.1. Variety: Offer a variety of food products to ensure a balanced diet. A mix of aquatic plants, leafy greens and vegetables is essential.

5.2. Freshness: Make sure the food you provide is fresh. Avoid faded or damaged items, as they can lead to health problems.

5.3. Frequency: Mud turtles should be fed daily or every other day, depending on their age and size.

5.4. Portion control: Avoid overeating. Provide an amount of food that the turtle can consume in a relatively short time.

5.5. Additional Calcium: Sprinkle foods periodically with a calcium supplement to ensure adequate calcium intake.

Section 6: Special Considerations

In some cases, you may encounter specific dietary requirements or considerations regarding mud turtles. Here are a few to keep in mind:

6.1. Age and height:

- Young turtles have different dietary needs than adults. Adjust the diet accordingly.
- Smaller turtles may need smaller, bite-sized foods.

6.2. Reproduction and laying:

Female mud turtles may need extra calcium during nesting season.

6.3. Hibernation:

If you are considering hibernating your mud turtle, consult a reptile veterinarian for advice on the fasting and hibernation regime.

Section 7: Observe and adjust diet

Observe your mud turtle's behavior and general condition regularly. This will help you make the necessary adjustments to his diet.

7.1. Weight and growth: Monitor the turtle's weight and growth to ensure it is developing properly.

7.2. Activity level: An active, alert turtle is generally a healthy turtle. If you notice lethargy or abnormal behavior, it may be a sign of health problems.

7.3. Stools and digestion: Pay attention to the quality of the turtle's stool. Diarrhea or unusual stool consistency may indicate eating problems.

7.4. Shell health: Inspect the shell for any signs of deformation, pyramiding, or soft spots, as these could be related to dietary issues.

Providing a good diet and understanding the dietary needs of mud turtles is an essential aspect of their care. By offering a diverse and balanced selection of aquatic plants, leafy greens and vegetables, you can help ensure their nutritional needs are met. Regular observation and adjustment of diet based on the behavior and health of the turtle is essential. Remember that each individual may have slightly different preferences and requirements. It is therefore essential to adapt the diet to the specific needs of your turtle for its well-being in captivity. Always consult a reptile veterinarian with any specific concerns or questions related to your mud turtle's diet and health.

Chapter 4
Care: Learn how to handle and care for mud turtles, including good hygiene practices.

Handling and caring for mud turtles requires knowledge, attention to detail and a commitment to their well-being. Mud turtles are unique reptiles that thrive when given proper care, which includes not only proper handling techniques, but also hygiene practices that keep them healthy. In this comprehensive guide, we'll explore the essential elements of handling and caring for mud turtles, from understanding their specific needs to ensuring their hygiene and health.

Section 1: Introduction to Mud Turtles

Before diving into the details of handling and care, it is essential to have a basic understanding of mud turtles.

1.1 About mud turtles

- Mud turtles, also known as African mud turtles or East African box turtles, are small to medium-sized turtles belonging to the genus Pelusios.

- They are semi-aquatic and found mainly in sub-Saharan Africa.
- Mud turtles are known for their distinctive domed shells and webbed feet, adapted to their aquatic lifestyle.
- Understanding their natural behavior and habitat is essential to providing proper care.

Section 2: Habitat and enclosure

Creating suitable habitat for mud turtles is the basis of their care.

2.1 Housing design

- Mud turtles need both aquatic and terrestrial spaces in their enclosure, as they spend time in the water and on land.
- Provide suitable substrate for digging and make sure there are hiding places and basking areas.

2.2 Temperature and lighting

- Maintain appropriate temperature gradients within the enclosure, including a warm basking area.

- Provide access to UVB lighting to support calcium metabolism.

2.3 Hygiene in the enclosure

- Clean and disinfect the enclosure regularly to prevent the buildup of waste and harmful bacteria.
- Change the water in the aquatic area and clean the water filter as necessary to maintain water quality.

Section 3: Handling Guidelines

Proper handling of mud turtles is important for their safety and comfort.

3.1 Frequency of handling

Mud turtles are generally not handled as frequently as some other pets. Limit handling to necessary tasks like health checks and habitat maintenance.

3.2 Gentle and slow approach

Approach your turtle calmly and gently. Avoid sudden movements or loud noises, which can stress them.

3.3 Handling technique

- Support the turtle's entire body when lifting it. Do not pick it up just by the shell, as this can be uncomfortable and potentially dangerous.
- Use both hands to lift the turtle, supporting its legs and keeping its body level.

3.4 Observation et respect

When handling, observe the turtle for any signs of stress or discomfort. If he seems distressed, gently return him to his enclosure.

Section 4: Dietary Requirements

Good nutrition is vital to the health of mud turtles.

4.1 Herbivorous diet

Mud turtles are herbivorous and feed primarily on plant matter, including aquatic plants, leafy greens, and some vegetables.

4.2 Balanced diet

Provide a variety of food items to ensure they receive a balanced diet. Avoid overfeeding and watch their weight.

4.3 Calcium and supplements

Sprinkle their food with a calcium supplement if necessary to ensure they get enough calcium.

Section 5: Hydration

Mud turtles absorb water through their skin, so access to clean water is essential.

5.1 Water area

Maintain a clean, shallow area of water for them to soak in and hydrate as needed.

5.2 Spray the case

Mist the soil and surroundings to maintain humidity levels and provide additional hydration.

Section 6: Health and veterinary care

Regular health checks and access to a reptile veterinarian are crucial to ensuring the well-being of mud turtles.

6.1 Signs of illness

Familiarize yourself with the signs of common reptile illnesses, such as loss of appetite, lethargy and changes in behavior.

6.2 Pest control

Mud turtles can be susceptible to internal and external parasites. Consult a reptile veterinarian for a parasite control plan.

6.3 Annual checks

Schedule annual checkups with a reptile veterinarian to monitor their overall health and address any potential problems.

Section 7: Social and Compatibility

Understanding the social needs and compatibility of mud turtles is important.

7.1 Social behavior

Some mud turtles are solitary, while others can tolerate the presence of conspecifics. Observe their behavior and interactions to determine the best arrangement.

7.2 Territorial behavior

Make sure there is enough space in the enclosure to avoid territorial conflicts if multiple turtles are kept together.

Section 8: Manipulation and Interaction for Enrichment

Mud turtles benefit from environmental enrichment and interaction.

8.1 Environmental enrichment

- Provide a stimulating environment with objects like plants, rocks and hiding places.
- Occasionally introduce them to new objects to explore.

8.2 Interactions

Although this is not a pet that craves social interaction, occasionally spending time near the enclosure can help it get used to human presence.

Section 9: Legal Considerations

Before acquiring a mud turtle, be aware of all legal regulations and restrictions regarding keeping them as pets in your area. Be sure to follow all local, state and national laws.

9.1 Legal ownership

Check the legality of owning a mud turtle as a pet in your area.

9.2 Permit requirements

In some areas, permits may be required to legally keep mud turtles.

The handling and care of mud turtles requires a dedicated and responsible approach. By understanding their specific needs, providing suitable habitat, providing adequate nutrition, and practicing good hygiene, you can ensure the well-being of these unique reptiles. Regular health checks, monitoring their behavior and following legal regulations are all integral to providing the best possible care. Always prioritize the well-being of your mud turtle and consult a reptile veterinarian with any specific concerns or questions related to their care and well-being.

Chapter 5
Health and Veterinary Care: Learn about common health concerns and how to find a reptile veterinarian for your mud turtle

Health and veterinary care are essential aspects of responsible pet ownership, and mud turtles are no exception. These unique reptiles require careful care to maintain their well-being. In this comprehensive guide, we'll cover various facets of health and veterinary care for mud turtles, including common health issues, preventative measures, and how to find a reptile veterinarian to ensure your pet's longevity and happiness.

Section 1: Introduction to Mud Turtle Health
Before exploring the specifics of veterinary health and care, it is crucial to understand the basics of mud turtle health and why it is essential to provide proper care.

1.1 The importance of health care
Maintaining the health of your mud turtle is crucial to its overall well-being and longevity.

Preventative measures and prompt attention to health problems can help prevent more serious problems.

1.2 Unique Health Needs of Mud Turtles

Mud turtles have specific health needs and considerations that differ from other reptiles and pets.

Section 2: Common Health Problems

Understanding the potential health issues that mud turtles may face is essential for rapid intervention and effective care.

2.1 Respiratory infections

Respiratory infections can occur if enclosure temperature and humidity levels are not properly maintained. Signs may include wheezing, runny nose, and difficulty breathing.

2.2 Hull problems

Shell problems, such as pyramiding (a condition in which the shell grows unevenly) or shell rot, can affect mud turtles. These problems are often due to poor nutrition, poor hygiene or unsuitable living conditions.

2.3 Parasites

Mud turtles can be susceptible to internal and external parasites, which can negatively impact their health. Symptoms may include weight loss, diarrhea and a dull appearance.

2.4 Metabolic bone disease (MBD)

MBD is a condition caused by a lack of calcium or an inappropriate calcium-to-phosphorus ratio in the diet. This can lead to weakened bones and deformities.

2.5 Skin and shell infections

Fungal or bacterial infections can affect the skin and shell, often due to unsanitary conditions or injury.

2.6 Stress-related problems

Mud turtles can become stressed due to mishandling, habitat changes, or environmental disturbances. Stress can lead to health problems and a weakened immune system.

2.7 Overgrown beak and nails

If a mud turtle's beak or nails become overgrown, it can lead to difficulty eating and moving. Regular pruning may be necessary.

2.8 Laying problems (females)

Female mud turtles may experience complications when laying eggs, such as retained eggs, which can be life-threatening.

2.9 Dehydration

Inadequate access to water can lead to dehydration, a common problem among mud turtles due to their reliance on skin absorption for hydration.

2.10 Parasitic flies (e.g. bottomy flies)

Certain types of flies can lay eggs on mud turtles, which can develop into parasitic larvae. Prompt egg removal is necessary to prevent infestation.

Section 3: Preventive measures

Preventing health problems is often more effective than treating them. Here are some preventive measures for mud turtle health:

3.1 Suitable habitat conditions

Maintain suitable housing conditions with appropriate temperature, humidity and sanitation practices.

3.2 Nutrition and diet

Make sure you eat a well-balanced diet that meets their nutritional needs, including adequate levels of calcium and phosphorus.

3.3 Hydration

Provide access to clean water for hydration, as mud turtles rely on skin absorption.

3.4 Regular health checks

Perform regular visual checks to quickly identify any changes or problems.

3.5 Environmental enrichment

Create a stimulating environment with hiding places, varied decor and safe objects to explore.

Section 4: Find a Reptile Veterinarian

Access to a qualified reptile veterinarian is essential to maintaining the health of your mud turtle. Finding a veterinarian who is an expert in reptile care is crucial.

4.1 Qualities of a reptile veterinarian

Look for a veterinarian experienced in treating reptiles and exotic animals. They must know the specific needs of mud turtles.

4.2 Ask for recommendations

Look for recommendations from other reptile owners, local pet stores, or online forums for reputable reptile veterinarians in your area.

4.3 Conduct interviews

Once you have identified potential reptile veterinarians, consider conducting interviews to ensure they are a good fit for your mud turtle's care.

4.4 Qualifications and experience

Check their credentials, such as as a licensed veterinarian, and ask about their experience with mud turtles.

4.5 Clinic and equipment

Visit the clinic or veterinary facility to assess its cleanliness, organization and equipment, which should be suitable for reptile care.

4.6 Availability

Check their availability and emergency services. Some health issues may require immediate attention.

4.7 Communications

Make sure you can communicate effectively with the veterinarian, and they can provide you with advice on caring for your mud turtle.

Section 5: Health checks and regular monitoring

Routine health checks and monitoring are essential to identify potential problems before they become serious.

5.1 Visual health checks

Inspect your mud turtle regularly for changes in behavior, appearance, or activity levels.

5.2 Recording observations

Keep track of your observations, including weight, eating habits, and any deviations from normal behavior.

5.3 Annual checks

Schedule annual checkups with your reptile veterinarian to assess overall health and address any concerns.

5.4 Parasite tests

Test regularly for parasites, as prevention and early intervention are essential to maintaining health.

Section 6: Emergency care and first aid

Preparing for emergencies is part of responsible pet ownership. Learn the basics of reptile first aid and have an emergency plan in place.

6.1 Common Reptile First Aid Supplies

Have basic first aid supplies on hand, such as sterile saline solution, clean rags, and a small container for soaking.

6.2 Emergency plan

Develop an emergency plan in case your mud turtle requires immediate medical attention. Know the location and contact details of the nearest reptile veterinarian.

6.3 Basic first aid techniques

Become familiar with basic reptile first aid techniques, such as how to clean and disinfect wounds, hydrate, and keep the turtle warm if it is cold.

Section 7: Medications and Treatments

If your mud turtle requires medication or treatment, follow your reptile veterinarian's instructions carefully.

7.1 Medication administration

Learn how to properly administer medications, including dosages and methods of administration.

7.2 Follow the veterinarian's advice

Always follow your veterinarian's advice regarding treatment and medication schedules.

7.3 Monitor progress

Monitor your mud turtle's progress regularly during treatment and report any changes or concerns to your veterinarian.

Health and veterinary care are essential components of responsible mud turtle ownership. Understanding common health problems, preventative measures, and how to find a qualified reptile veterinarian ensures your pet receives the best care possible. By taking a proactive approach to your mud turtle's health, you will enjoy many years of companionship and the satisfaction of providing a safe and healthy environment for your unique reptilian friend. Always prioritize the well-being of your mud turtle and do not hesitate to consult a professional veterinarian if necessary.

Chapter 6
Legal Considerations for Keeping Mud Turtles as Pets

Many people want to keep mud turtles as pets because of their intriguing behaviors and captivating personalities. However, before acquiring a mud turtle as a pet, it is essential to understand the legal regulations and restrictions in your area, as these can vary greatly from location to location. This chapter will delve deeper into the legal considerations associated with keeping mud turtles as pets, exploring the following key aspects:

Overview of Mud Turtles

Before we get into the legalities, it's important to understand what mud turtles are. Mud turtles are a group of small aquatic or semi-aquatic turtles that primarily inhabit muddy or swampy areas. They are known for their distinctive appearance, which includes webbed feet and a dome-shaped shell. Different species of mud turtles can be found in various regions of the world, from North America to Asia and Africa.

Why people choose mud turtles as pets

Mud turtles attract pet lovers for several reasons. Their relatively small size, interesting behavior, and relatively simple care requirements make them attractive options for those looking to keep a pet reptile. Additionally, their unique habitat preferences and appearance contribute to their popularity as pets.

Legal regulations and restrictions

When considering keeping mud turtles as pets, it is essential to be aware of the legal regulations and restrictions in your area. These laws are in place to protect wildlife and ensure the well-being of these creatures. Specific regulations may vary from jurisdiction to jurisdiction and it is essential to be well informed.

Federal laws: In many countries, including the United States, federal laws govern the possession and trade of wild animals. These laws are designed to protect native and non-native species and prevent illegal wildlife trafficking. Mud turtles may be covered by these regulations.

State or provincial laws: In addition to federal laws, states or provinces often have their own regulations regarding keeping wild animals as pets. These laws may be more restrictive or permissive than federal laws and may require permits or licenses.

Local regulations: Some municipalities or local governments may have specific ordinances or regulations related to the keeping of exotic animals, including mud turtles. It is important to research and understand these local laws, as they can vary widely.

Protected species and conservation status

Some mud turtle species may be protected due to their conservation status. For example, the Sonoran mud turtle, a species native to the southwestern United States, is considered a threatened species under the U.S. Endangered Species Act. This means that the possession, sale or trade of this species may be subject to strict regulations.

Permits and licenses

In some areas, acquiring a permit or license may be necessary to legally keep mud turtles as pets. These permits often come with specific requirements, such as providing suitable habitat and demonstrating a commitment to animal welfare. Obtaining the necessary permits is a crucial step in remaining compliant with the law.

Restrictions d'importation et d'exportation

The import and export of mud turtles across international borders may be subject to strict regulations and documentation requirements. These measures are in place to prevent illegal wildlife trade and protect the species' natural habitats.

Health and safety concerns

Many legal regulations regarding keeping mud turtles as pets are driven by concerns about the animals' health and safety. Reptiles can carry diseases that can be transmitted to humans, and improper care can lead to health problems for the animals. Laws often include provisions to ensure appropriate standards of care and hygiene.

Penalties for non-compliance

It is crucial to understand the penalties for non-compliance with wildlife regulations. Consequences for illegally owning or trading mud turtles can include fines, confiscation of the animals, and even criminal prosecution. Being aware of these penalties can help potential pet owners make informed decisions.

Rescue and rehabilitation centers

In some cases, individuals may encounter injured or abandoned mud turtles and wish to provide them with care. Before taking in such animals, it is important to know any legal requirements or obligations associated with wildlife rescue and rehabilitation.

Ethical considerations

Beyond legal regulations, ethical considerations should also play an important role in deciding whether or not to keep mud turtles as pets. It is essential to evaluate whether it is in the best interests of the animals to keep them in captivity and whether there are suitable alternatives, such as supporting conservation efforts or preserving habitat.

Education and awareness

The key to responsible pet ownership is education and awareness. Prospective mud turtle owners should thoroughly research the species' natural history, care requirements, and potential legal obligations before bringing one into their home.

In conclusion, the legal considerations for keeping mud turtles as pets are multiple and can vary greatly depending on your location. Understanding and complying with these regulations is essential not only to avoid legal problems, but also to ensure the well-being and conservation of these unique reptiles. It is advisable to consult local wildlife authorities, seek legal advice if necessary, and prioritize ethical and responsible pet ownership when considering mud turtles as pets. Always remember that the main goal is to provide a safe and suitable environment for these fascinating creatures. By integrating the above points into one comprehensive article, we have covered the legal regulations and restrictions associated with keeping mud turtles as pets. ensuring that potential pet owners are well informed and prepared to take action. responsible decisions. It is essential to recognize that these regulations are in place to protect both the welfare of animals and the integrity of their natural habitats. By being aware of and respecting these legal considerations, we can contribute to the conservation of these unique reptiles while enjoying their presence as pets.

Chapter 7
Enrichment and Activities for Mud Turtles: Promoting a Happy, Healthy Pet

Mud turtles belong to the Kinosternidae family and can be found in various parts of the world. These semi-aquatic or aquatic turtles are often recognized by their webbed feet, dome-shaped shells, and their preference for muddy or swampy habitats. Mud turtles come in several different species, each with their own characteristics and requirements.

The importance of enrichment for mud turtles
Enriching mud turtles is essential for several reasons. Although they are not as active as some other pets, these reptiles still need stimulation to maintain their physical and mental health. Enrichment activities can help prevent boredom, encourage natural behaviors, and promote overall well-being. When mud turtles are kept in captivity, it is our responsibility as pet owners to ensure that they have a fulfilling life.

Physical and mental stimulation

1. Outdoor speakers

One of the best ways to physically and mentally stimulate mud turtles is to create an outdoor enclosure for them. Mud turtles love to bask in the sun and explore their surroundings. A secure outdoor enclosure with access to sunlight allows them to engage in natural behaviors such as digging and foraging. Make sure the enclosure is leak-proof and provides protection from predators.

2. Dig for opportunities

Mud turtles are avid diggers and can spend a lot of time burying themselves in the substrate. Providing a deep layer of suitable substrate, such as mud or dirt, in their enclosure allows them to exhibit this natural behavior. Hide treats or toys in the substrate to encourage digging and foraging.

3. Water Characteristics

Since mud turtles are semi-aquatic, water play in their enclosure can be rewarding. A small, shallow pond or flat of water where they can bathe and swim is beneficial. Make sure the water is clean and the depth is appropriate for the turtle's size, as they are not good swimmers.

4. Climbing Structures

While mud turtles live primarily on the ground, providing low, sturdy climbing structures can be empowering. These structures can mimic natural obstacles they might encounter in nature and encourage exploration.

5. Hiding places

Create hiding places within the enclosure using logs, rocks or artificial caves. Mud turtles often seek shelter when they feel stressed or need a break. Having these places available can therefore reduce stress and provide comfort.

Diet and foraging enrichment

1. Foraging Toys

Introducing foraging toys can be a great way to stimulate a mud turtle's natural instincts. These toys can be filled with small amounts of food, such as leafy greens or pieces of vegetables. The turtle must work to extract the food, thus promoting mental engagement.

2. Varied diet

Provide a diverse and balanced diet to keep your mud turtle occupied. Although they have their favorite foods, like aquatic plants and insects, providing them with different options makes mealtime interesting. However, always make sure the foods are safe and suitable for turtles.

3. Occasional live prey

Mud turtles, like many other reptiles, can benefit from occasional live prey, such as small insects. Hunting and capturing live prey can be mentally stimulating and add variety to their diet.

Environmental enrichment

1. Seasonal changes

Simulating seasonal changes in temperature and daylight hours can be enriching for mud turtles. This can be done by gradually adjusting the lighting and temperature settings in their enclosure to mimic changes in nature.

2. Rotating decor

Periodically changing the decor and layout of the enclosure can prevent habituation and boredom. This simple adjustment can pique a mud turtle's curiosity and keep them engaged.

Social enrichment

1. Interactions sociales

Although mud turtles are not inherently social animals, they can benefit from gentle interactions with their owners. Being present in their enclosure and observing their behavior can provide a sense of camaraderie.

2. Several turtles

If you have multiple mud turtles, allowing them to interact with each other can be rewarding. However, it is essential to monitor their interactions to ensure that they do not become aggressive.

Surveillance and security

While enrichment is crucial to a mud turtle's well-being, it is essential to monitor its behavior and safety during these activities. Make sure all outdoor enclosures are secure to prevent escape or exposure to predators. In addition, always provide access to fresh water and a suitable resting area.

In conclusion, providing enrichment and activities for mud turtles is an integral part of responsible pet ownership. Although these reptiles are not as active or social as some other pets, they have specific needs and behaviors that must be considered. By creating a stimulating environment that mimics its natural habitat, providing a varied diet, and ensuring its safety and well-being, you can promote the happiness and health of your mud turtle. Remember that each mud turtle may have individual preferences and needs. It is therefore essential to observe its behavior and adapt your enrichment accordingly to provide the best possible quality of life for these unique reptiles. It is essential to approach mud turtle enrichment with a sense of responsibility and care. These creatures rely on their owners to create an environment that allows them to thrive and display natural behaviors. By incorporating the enrichment and activity methods discussed, you can ensure that your mud turtle leads a fulfilling and healthy life as a cherished pet.

Chapter 8
Mud Turtle Lifespan and Size: A Complete Guide

Lifespan of Mud Turtles

The lifespan of mud turtles can vary greatly depending on a variety of factors, including species, care, and environmental conditions. Understanding these factors is essential to ensuring the long-term well-being of these reptiles.

1. Species variation

Different species of mud turtles have varying lifespans. Here are some examples:

Common mud turtle (Kinosternon subrubrum): This North American species has an average lifespan of 40 to 55 years in the wild. When kept in captivity with proper care, they can live even longer.

Yellow mud turtle (Kinosternon flavescens): This species found in Central America and Mexico can live up to 50 years or more.

Striped mud turtle (Kinosternon baurii): Native to the southeastern United States, this species typically has a lifespan of 25 to 30 years, but with excellent care it can live longer.

Sonoran mud turtle (Kinosternon sonoriense): This species found in the southwestern United States and Mexico is considered endangered and has a relatively long lifespan of up to 40 years or more.

2. Lifespan in captivity or in the wild

Mud turtles kept in captivity generally have a longer lifespan than those living in the wild. In captivity, they are protected from natural predators and have access to a constant food supply. Proper care, including adequate diet, housing and veterinary care, is essential to ensure a long and healthy life for mud turtles in captivity.

3. Environmental factors

Environmental conditions play an important role in the lifespan of mud turtles. Temperature, humidity and access to clean water are essential to their well-being. Turtles kept in environments that closely mimic their natural habitat tend to live longer and healthier lives.

4. Diet and Nutrition

A well-balanced diet is essential to the longevity of mud turtles. Good nutrition supports their growth and overall health. A diet consisting of a variety of vegetables, aquatic plants, and, for some species, occasional live prey is ideal. A diet rich in calcium is crucial to maintaining the health of their shell.

5. Veterinary care

Regular check-ups and prompt medical attention when needed are essential to ensure mud turtles live long and healthy lives. Unresolved health issues can have a significant impact on their lifespan.

Mud Turtle Size

Mud turtles vary in size and it is important to understand their growth patterns to determine appropriate care and habitat needs.

1. Size of newborns

Mud turtle hatchlings are relatively small and fragile. They are usually about 1.5 to 2 inches (3.8 to 5 cm) in length at birth. Due to their small size, they are more vulnerable to predators and providing them with a secure environment is essential at this stage.

2. Adult size

The adult size of mud turtles varies depending on the species. Here are some examples:

Common mud turtle (Kinosternon subrubrum): Adults typically reach lengths of 4 to 5 inches (10 to 13 cm), with females often being slightly larger than males.

Yellow mud turtle (Kinosternon flavescens): Adult yellow mud turtles can reach 5 to 6 inches (13 to 15 cm) in length.

Striped mud turtle (Kinosternon baurii): Adults are relatively small, with lengths of 3.5 to 4 inches (9 to 10 cm).

Sonoran mud turtle (Kinosternon sonoriense): Adults of this species are larger, reaching lengths of 6 to 7 inches (15 to 18 cm).

3. Growth rate

The growth rate of mud turtles can be influenced by a variety of factors, including diet, temperature, and general care. In general, these turtles grow slowly compared to some other reptiles. It may take several years before they reach adult size.

4. Gender differences

In some species, there may be differences in size between males and females. In many cases, females are slightly larger than males. These size differences are important to consider if you plan to keep multiple mud turtles together.

Factors influencing size and lifespan

Several factors can influence the size and lifespan of mud turtles. These factors are essential to consider when caring for these reptiles:

1. Genetics

Genetics play a role in determining the potential size and lifespan of an individual mud turtle. Certain genetic variations can result in larger or smaller individuals within a species.

2. Diet and Nutrition

The diet provided to mud turtles has a direct impact on their growth and overall health. A diet rich in essential nutrients and tailored to their specific species is crucial to reaching their potential size and living a long life.

3. Environmental conditions

Maintaining appropriate environmental conditions, including temperature, humidity and access to clean water, is vital to their well-being and can influence their growth and longevity.

4. Veterinary care

Regular veterinary checks and prompt treatment of any health problems are essential to ensure that mud turtles can grow to their potential size and live long, healthy lives.

In conclusion, understanding the lifespan and size of mud turtles is crucial to providing them with proper care and ensuring their well-being. These reptiles vary in size depending on the species and can live for a relatively long time, especially when kept in captivity with proper care. Factors such as genetics, diet, environmental conditions and access to veterinary care play an important role in determining their size and lifespan. Whether you are considering mud turtles as pets or are simply interested in these fascinating creatures, it is essential to recognize the factors that influence their growth and longevity. By providing them with a suitable environment, a balanced diet and regular health care, you can help ensure that mud turtles lead fulfilling and healthy lives. Remember that each mud turtle is unique and proper care tailored to their individual needs is key to their well-being and longevity.

Chapter 9
Conservation and Ethical Considerations: Promoting Responsible Pet Ownership and Protecting Endangered Species

Conservation and ethical considerations play a vital role in our responsibility as stewards of the natural world. As we share our lives with diverse species, including pets, it is essential to recognize the importance of responsible pet ownership and the broader imperative to preserve endangered species. This article will delve deeper into the importance of these two aspects, highlighting the ethical and practical reasons to safeguard our planet's biodiversity.

The importance of biodiversity

Biodiversity refers to the variety of life forms on Earth, including species, genetic diversity and ecosystems. It is a fundamental part of the health and resilience of our planet. Biodiversity offers a multitude of benefits, such as:

Ecosystem Service: Biodiversity is essential for the proper functioning of ecosystems, including pollination, nutrient cycling and pest control. These services support agriculture, food production and human well-being.

Medicine and innovation: Many pharmaceutical products and advances in various fields come from the study of biodiversity. The genetic diversity found in different species holds potential for future innovations and discoveries.

Cultural and aesthetic value: Biodiversity enriches human culture, providing aesthetic pleasure, inspiration for art and literature, and spiritual significance for many cultures.

Resilience and adaptation: A diverse ecosystem is more resilient to environmental changes. In the face of climate change and other challenges, biodiversity can improve adaptability.

The role of responsible pet ownership

Responsible pet ownership is an essential aspect of ethical and practical considerations regarding biodiversity and conservation. It encompasses a set of principles and practices that ensure the well-being of pets and minimize their impact on ecosystems.

1. Proper care and wellness

Responsible pet ownership begins with providing proper care and welfare to pets. This involves meeting their basic needs for nutrition, housing, health care and social interaction. Ensuring animals are healthy and happy promotes ethical treatment and responsible guardianship.

2. Species-specific knowledge

Understanding the specific needs of an animal species is crucial. Different animals require different levels of care, including diet, housing conditions and social interactions. Good knowledge is fundamental to ensuring that pets thrive in captivity.

3. Prevent overpopulation

Overpopulation of companion animals, particularly dogs and cats, is a significant problem with implications for both animal welfare and conservation. Spaying and neutering are essential practices to prevent overpopulation, reduce euthanasia rates, and combat the impact of wild animals on native wildlife.

4. Ethical breeding and adoption

For people interested in raising pets, ethical practices that prioritize animal health and welfare are paramount. Adoption from animal shelters and rescue organizations is an ethical choice that helps reduce the demand for commercially bred animals.

5. Ban exotic and invasive animals

Some exotic and invasive species pose serious threats to ecosystems. Responsible pet ownership includes regulations that restrict or prohibit the keeping of species that may escape into the wild and disrupt natural habitats.

6. Support conservation initiatives

Responsible pet owners can contribute to conservation efforts by supporting organizations and initiatives that work to protect species and their natural habitats. This may include financial contributions and volunteering.

The impact of irresponsible pet ownership

Irresponsible pet ownership has a variety of negative consequences, including:

Abandon: Careless or ill-prepared owners may abandon their pets, leading to suffering and overpopulation.

Invasive species: Some pets, when released or escaped, can become invasive and harm native wildlife. Examples include Burmese pythons in the Florida Everglades and wild cats around the world.

Wildlife trade: The illegal trade in exotic animals contributes to the decimation of wild populations, thus threatening species with extinction.

Destruction of habitat: The demand for exotic animals can lead to habitat destruction and deforestation in countries of origin, impacting ecosystems.

The importance of conserving endangered species
Conservation efforts are essential to safeguarding endangered species and preserving the planet's biodiversity. Threatened species are those that are at high risk of extinction in the wild. The importance of conservation becomes evident when considering the following:

1. Ecosystem health

Every species, no matter how small or inconspicuous, plays a role in the complex web of life. When a species disappears, it can disrupt ecosystems, leading to imbalances and cascading effects. The loss of a single species can impact the abundance and distribution of many others.

2. Loss of biodiversity

The extinction of a species represents a permanent loss of biodiversity. Biodiversity provides insurance against environmental change and provides options for future adaptations. Preserving it is equivalent to preserving our biological heritage.

3. Scientific discovery

Species that remain to be studied could hold secrets and solutions to problems in human health, agriculture and the environment. Preserving biodiversity is vital for future discoveries and innovations.

4. Moral and ethical responsibility

Humans have an ethical responsibility to protect and conserve species and their habitats. It reflects our recognition of the intrinsic value of all forms of life and our commitment to stewardship.

5. Economic value

Biodiversity contributes to various economic sectors, including tourism, agriculture and pharmaceuticals. Species loss can have economic repercussions, making conservation an economically sound choice.

6. Ecosystem services

Endangered species often provide ecosystem services. For example, predators control prey populations, preventing overgrazing and ecosystem degradation. The disappearance of these species can lead to imbalances with ecological and economic consequences.

Conservation methods

Conservation efforts employ a variety of strategies and methods to protect endangered species and their habitats:

Protection de l'habitat: Preserving the natural habitats of endangered species is often the most effective method of conservation. This may involve the creation of protected areas, such as national parks and wildlife reserves.

Species Recovery Programs: These programs focus on breeding and reintroduction of endangered species into the wild. They may include captive breeding, habitat restoration and monitoring.

Regulatory measures: Regulations and laws can prohibit hunting, trade, and habitat destruction that harm endangered species. These measures can be national or international, such as the Convention on International Trade in Endangered Species of Wild Fauna and Flora (CITES).

Education and Awareness: It is crucial to educate the public about the importance of biodiversity and the threats to endangered species. Awareness campaigns can inspire support for conservation efforts.

Scientific Research: Continued research is essential to understanding threatened species and developing effective conservation strategies.

Community Involvement: Engaging local communities in conservation efforts can be very effective. It encourages support for conservation measures and fosters a sense of stewardship.

Collaboration internationale : Many endangered species migrate across borders. International cooperation is often necessary to effectively protect these species.

The role of responsible pet ownership in conservation

Responsible pet ownership can intersect with conservation efforts in several ways:

Protection de l'habitat: Responsible pet owners can support habitat protection initiatives and help preserve ecosystems where many species, including their pets' wildlife relatives, reside.

Avoid exotic animals: By not acquiring exotic animals that may have been obtained illegally or contribute to the trade in endangered species, responsible pet owners help reduce the demand for these animals.

Promote ethical breeding: Ethical breeding practices prioritize animal health and welfare. Responsible pet breeders can be models of ethical practices that benefit all animals, not just pets.

Support conservation organizations: Responsible pet owners can financially support and volunteer with conservation organizations that work to protect endangered species and their habitats.

Education and Awareness: Pet owners can educate themselves and others about the importance of conservation and responsible pet ownership. This awareness can lead to more informed decisions and greater support for conservation efforts.

In conclusion, conservation and ethical considerations are interrelated aspects of our responsibility as stewards of the planet's biodiversity. Responsible pet ownership not only ensures the well-being of our pets, but also mitigates the negative impact of pets on ecosystems and wildlife. Additionally, conservation efforts are crucial to protecting endangered species, preserving biodiversity, and maintaining the health and resilience of our planet. As individuals, communities and societies, we must recognize the ethical and practical importance of these responsibilities. We must make informed choices as pet owners, support conservation initiatives, and advocate for measures that protect our natural world. In doing so, we contribute to a more sustainable and harmonious coexistence with the diverse forms of life that share our planet.

Chapter 10
Personal Experiences with Mud Turtles: The Joys and Challenges of Keeping Them as Pets

Mud turtles, also known as mud turtles, have found their place as beloved pets in the hearts of many reptile lovers. These unique creatures offer intriguing behaviors, charming personalities, and insight into the world of semi-aquatic reptiles. In this article, we will delve into the personal experiences of pet owners who have had the privilege of sharing their lives with mud turtles, gaining insight into the joys and challenges of keeping these remarkable reptiles as pets of company.

The fascination with mud turtles

Mud turtles belong to the Kinosternidae family and are known for their distinctive features, including webbed feet and a dome-shaped shell. Although they may not be as famous as some other reptile species, mud turtles have attracted a devoted following among those who appreciate their unique attributes.

Joys of keeping mud turtles

Quirky Personalities: Mud turtles have charming personalities that can be endearing to their owners. They exhibit various behaviors, such as digging, basking, and interacting with their environment, which add character to their daily routines.

Fascinating behaviors: Observing the natural behaviors of mud turtles is one of the main joys of owning them. From their digging and burrowing habits to their swimming and basking activities, they provide a window into the lives of semi-aquatic reptiles.

Low maintenance: Compared to some other pets, mud turtles are relatively low maintenance. They do not require social interaction or constant attention, making them suitable for people who enjoy the presence of a pet without needing high levels of interaction.

Educational Opportunities: Mud turtles provide valuable educational opportunities, both for their owners and for those lucky enough to learn about them. Understanding their unique adaptations and behaviors can be a gateway to appreciating the wonders of the natural world.

Longevity: Mud turtles are known for their impressive lifespans, often living for several decades. This longevity allows owners to enjoy their companionship for many years.

The Challenges of Raising Mud Turtles

Specialized Housing Needs: Mud turtles require specific habitat conditions, including access to water and land. Meeting these needs can be challenging and may involve creating semi-aquatic enclosures.

Regulatory considerations: In some areas, keeping mud turtles as pets may be subject to legal regulations and restrictions. Understanding and following these laws is essential to responsible ownership.

Consistent care requirements: Although mud turtles are low maintenance in some respects, they still require constant care, including maintaining appropriate temperature and humidity levels, a proper diet, and access to clean water.

Health problems : Like all pets, mud turtles can experience health problems. Finding a qualified reptile veterinarian who can diagnose and treat these problems can be a challenge in some areas.

Long-term commitment: Mud turtles have an impressive lifespan, meaning owning one is a long-term commitment. Potential owners should be prepared to care for their pet for several decades.

Personal Stories of Mud Turtle Owners

Let's dive into the personal experiences of mud turtle owners to better understand the joys and challenges of keeping these unique reptiles as pets.

Story 1: Sarah's connection with her mud turtle

Sarah, a reptile enthusiast, shares her story of acquiring a mud turtle named Sam. She describes how Sam's bizarre behaviors and semi-aquatic nature immediately attracted her. "Sam is such an interesting character," she says. "I love watching him swim and dig, and he seems to have a knack for finding the most comfortable spots in his enclosure." Sarah admits that while mud turtles have brought her much joy, their habitat requirements can be a challenge. "Creating the right environment for Sam was a learning experience," she admits. "Maintaining water quality and providing the right amount of land space took some trial and error, but it was worth it to see it thrive."

Story 2: Mark's journey with several mud turtles
Mark is a dedicated mud turtle owner with several of these reptiles in his care. He shares his experiences with the joys of seeing them interact with each other and with their habitat. "I have several mud turtles in a large outdoor enclosure," says Mark. "It's fascinating to observe their social dynamics and the way they shape their territories." Mark also highlights the importance of responsible pet ownership, especially when it comes to invasive species. "I made sure to only conserve native species and create a safe and secure habitat for them," he notes. "We must be responsible managers of these animals and their environment."

Story 3: Challenges and Rewards with Lily's Mud Turtle

Lily recounts her experiences with a rescued mud turtle named Franklin. "Franklin came to me after being neglected by his previous owner," she says. "He had health issues and a lot of stress when I first got him." Lily describes the challenges of restoring Franklin's health, including finding a reptile veterinarian and creating a suitable enclosure. Despite the initial difficulties, Lily found great satisfaction in providing a better life for Franklin. "His progress has been remarkable," she adds. "It's a testament to the resilience of these creatures, and it's incredibly rewarding to see it healthy and thriving."

Practical advice from experienced owners

Experienced mud turtle owners often have valuable information and advice to offer those considering these reptiles as pets. Here are some practical tips:

Research species: Mud turtles come in different species, each with their own specific requirements. Research the species you are interested in carefully to ensure you can meet their needs.

Habitat counts: Pay particular attention to the design and maintenance of the habitat. It should include both a water area and a land area, with suitable substrate and hiding places.

Consult a veterinarian: Finding a veterinarian experienced in caring for reptiles is crucial. Regular checkups and immediate attention to health problems are essential for your pet's long-term health.

Maintain good nutrition: Offer a balanced diet adapted to the species. A varied menu of vegetables, aquatic plants and, for some species, occasional live prey is beneficial.

Legality and conservation: Be aware of the legal regulations regarding keeping mud turtles as pets in your area. Additionally, consider the conservation status of the species you are interested in and support ethical sources.

Community and Education: Join online forums and communities where experienced owners share knowledge and offer support. Learning from the experiences of others can be invaluable.

Long-term commitment: Be aware that mud turtles have a long lifespan, so consider the commitment you are making. They will be part of your life for many years.

The personal experiences of mud turtle owners offer insight into the joys and challenges of keeping these unique reptiles as pets. From the endearing behaviors and personalities of mud turtles to the responsibilities and challenges of providing proper habitat and care, their stories reflect the depth of connection that can be made with these remarkable creatures. Owning a mud turtle requires a combination of dedication, knowledge and a true passion for reptiles. The experiences of these pet owners highlight the need for responsible pet ownership and ethical considerations, while celebrating the rewarding journey of sharing life with mud turtles. As with any pet, the key to a successful and fulfilling relationship with a mud turtle lies in education, commitment, and a deep appreciation for the wonders of the natural world.